Words
FOR YOUR
Wedding

THE
WEDDING SERVICE
BOOK

Words
FOR YOUR
Wedding

DAVID GLUSKER
&
PETER MISNER

HarperSanFrancisco
A Division of HarperCollinsPublishers

WORDS FOR YOUR WEDDING. Copyright © 1983 by David L. Glusker, Peter L. Misner and Kennebec Press. Copyright © 1986 by David L. Glusker and Peter L. Misner. All rights reserved. Printed in the United States of America. No part of this book may be used or reproduced in any manner whatsoever without written permission except in the case of brief quotations embodied in critical articles and reviews. For information address HarperCollins Publishers, 10 East 53rd Street, New York, NY 10022.

First Harper & Row paperback edition published in 1986 by arrangement with Lance Tapley, Publisher.

Designed by Abby Trudeau.

Library of Congress Cataloging-in-Publication Data
Main entry under title:

Words for your wedding.

    1. Marrige service—Texts.   I. Glusker, David Lowell, 1938–   .   Misner, Peter, 1933–
[BV199.M3W67 1986]   265'.5   85-45353
ISBN 0-06-063131-7 (pbk.)
ISBN 0-06-063132-5 (retailers only: pbk.)

93　94　95　CWI　15　14　13　12

Acknowledgments

Our deep gratitude is expressed to our wives Esther and Susan. Special thanks go to Jan Roy, who spent countless hours preparing material and typing; to Nancy Miner, who added her typing skills to the final manuscript; to Dot Washburn, who helped us throughout the project; and to W. Richard Souza for his contribution of an "affirmation of the community." A final word of gratitude goes to Gary Vencill for his encouragement and counsel throughout our work.

Preface: A Wish

"In the beginning was the Word..."

Welcome to the excitement and challenge of planning the service for your wedding.

For many months or years one of your private dreams may have been the picture of your wedding day and of the service at its center. It may be that you have been a participant in a wedding and have filed away a memory from that time — an action, a phrase, an idea — that seemed to draw everything together. You thought: "Someday I'd like that to happen at *my* wedding."

Or it may be that you have not given the service itself much thought until now and are wondering where to begin. In either case, this book is for you. It is also for clergymen and -women, parents and others involved in planning a wedding. We have prepared it to be *the* reference book on the words spoken at a wedding.

However long it may be until the wedding date, you will find there are a hundred details you never expected to have to consider. You may discover that you feel pressures and even anxiety about the wedding. There will be decisions about who will be in the wedding party, what they should wear, where the reception will be and so on. The service itself — the words spoken — may become a secondary concern.

If this happens, it is unfortunate. The words spoken will be what unites you and your intended. They are the central action of this wonderful drama. This book has been written to show the importance these ceremonial words have. It also intends to help you become more involved with them by presenting a range of words for you to choose from. A carefully planned service will reflect your deepest feelings and intentions.

All the details will fall into a true perspective when you remember that the wedding is an experience of worship. Careful planning of the wedding service will help you and the person officiating create an occasion rich with reverential meaning both for you and for the friends you invite to take part. A day you will never forget. Words you will never forget. That is our wish for you.

the authors

Contents

Part I
First Things

The Wedding Service Past and Present

The spoken ceremony of a wedding is a central rite in the life of a man and a woman. It is a formal way of marking a beginning, a commitment, a change of relationships within a family and a new family within the human community. It is a time for a festive gathering of family and friends as well as a very personal experience for the bride and groom.

The words spoken are like those that have bound human relationships for generations. Words like those you will be using in your wedding ceremony have been heard in cathedrals and tiny chapels, in homes and gardens and sometimes in very exotic settings. Always the purpose has been the same: the marking of this important new relationship, marriage, which unites kings and queens, the wealthy and the powerful as well as people who live in the simplest of circumstances. The words are important for their history in addition to their specific meaning for you in the marriage you are now anticipating.

There is a special stature to the words of the traditional wedding service, for as they are spoken everyone present will remember times these words have been heard before. The familiarity of everyone with them makes a powerful statement about the importance of the occasion. And it reminds the couple that they are embarking on a road which is well established in our history and culture.

A view increasingly prevalent in recent years is that a wedding should reflect more of the personal vision and commitment of the bride and groom. Marriage is based in the life of the community and its history, but it is also a distinctly personal experience. *This* wedding has never happened before.

The past several decades have seen many influences come to bear on wedding ceremonies. Second marriages are frequent. Many couples have lived together before deciding to marry. Wide varieties of experience affect decisions to consult a member of the clergy about a wedding service.

Some couples create their own service. Such ceremonies, rooted in the life of the couple, are often especially beautiful and significant. The very process of writing vows and other words of covenant is important to the couple.

Taking into account all these changes, the authors felt it would be useful to create a book which would express the diversity and richness of contemporary wedding services as well as contain the traditional service. As ministers who have officiated at innumerable weddings, we know that encouraging couples to choose the various parts of their service from a variety of services presented to them can make a wedding extremely meaningful. We also recognize that several denominations have no formal or even commonly accepted words for weddings; the usefulness of this book for them should be apparent.

A few Protestant denominations recently have made efforts to enrich their marriage service. The United Church of Christ, the United Methodist Church, the American Lutheran Church, the Episcopal Church and the United Church of

Canada are among these. This book draws from these five denominations as well as from an older Protestant service (referred to as the traditional service) which has been and still is the basis of words used by many other denominations. In the book also are services written by the authors. These are offered in an effort to provide alternatives in language or to approach a particular function from a fresh perspective.

This is a manual that will be used for the most part by couples and by the clergy in planning a wedding service. It is not a book about weddings, although thoughts about the subject can be found throughout. The format has been chosen in an attempt to encourage creativity on the part of couples planning weddings. The first chapter tells you how to use the book.

We have also created a loose-leaf version of the book in a ring binder to make it as convenient as possible for the person officiating to use the chosen materials at the service. Please see the back pages of the book for more information on this.

The words of a wedding can be spoken not only in a church. Many couples, of course, automatically think of the church in which they have participated in the worship of God with family and friends. The church building may be a familiar landmark in their life in the community. It may be filled with reminders of other celebrations — weddings, baptisms, funerals. The church may be the most appropriate setting for their wedding ceremony.

The worship of God, however, has never been limited to the community's recognized holy places. Locations other than a church may provide for a couple a feeling of holiness. They may be led to choose a quiet glen, the backyard of a beloved home, a scenic spot beside the water. The couple as well as the clergy carry responsibility for ensuring that the place which is chosen for the wedding will be in harmony with the spirit of the worship service.

Whether the ceremony is to take place in a church or in some other setting, it will be important for the bride and groom, as well as for the officiating person, to do everything possible to ensure that the reverence of the ceremony is felt without distraction. When a ceremony is held out-of-doors, some care will need to be taken to make the guests comfortable — perhaps with a shelter available in case of unsettled weather. It is also important that the wedding take place where there will be no distraction from traffic noises or other sounds which would take people's attention from where it should be.

Perhaps a word should also be said about photography during the wedding ceremony. The careful recording of this beautiful, fleeting moment is important, but it should never become distracting in the way it takes place. Professional photographers are usually sensitive to the ceremony and are careful to move in an unobtrusive manner as they do their work. Usually the photographer will have a camera positioned for the processional and recessional and be able to take a "long shot" without flash across the congregation during the course of the ceremony. The photographer need not take pictures beyond this during the service itself. Any close-ups can be taken when the formal pictures of the wedding party are made at the conclusion of the wedding.

Guests who bring cameras to the wedding should be invited by the ushers, prior to the service, to refrain from taking pictures during the ceremony in order not to disturb the service. Of course, it goes without saying that members of the wedding party will never carry cameras nor take pictures during the wedding.

How to Use This Book

As a couple reflects on their impending wedding ceremony, they should first consider both the content and the tone of the statement which they wish the service to make to each other and to family and friends. They then should choose the order of worship — the sequence of the service — and, after that, the particular words in each part of the service which will best enable them to realize their objective.

The various services offered in this book may be an adequate range of options. Or the couple may choose to write an order and words of their own; to help in this, a chapter has been included containing suggestions about how best to write a service.

A couple likely will want to choose some parts from one service and other parts from a second or third. For example, the simple order of worship from the traditional service may be chosen as the core of their service, but the couple also may wish to have an opening prayer, the reading of a scripture lesson, a meditation by the clergy and special music. This is perfectly acceptable, a reasonable thing to do. This book suggests that no one service automatically fits every situation. Methodists may decide that they prefer certain Lutheran ways of saying certain parts of the wedding service, and vice versa. Construct a service that will be best for you.

The decisions should result in an outline on paper containing specific references to the various passages listed. These choices should then be reviewed with the officiating clergyman or -woman to insure that the service is appropriate and in keeping with the couple's objectives. The minister may make suggestions regarding the order of worship itself or the addition or deletion of particular alternatives within the service.

Generally, the ceremony begins with a musical prelude, although this is quite optional. Instrumental or vocal music can handsomely enrich the wedding. However, some kinds of music are not appropriate for a wedding service. It is important that music be discussed prior to the wedding with the officiating minister or priest and, of course, with the organist or other musicians.

Readings from sources other than the Bible can also strengthen a service. Be conscious, however, of the necessity of the readings being consistent with the personal and social significance of the wedding.

A wedding meditation or sermon can become an important part of the service. It is a personal word spoken by the person officiating to the couple as well as to all who attend. The couple may suggest a theme or idea which they would like to have expressed by the minister.

People other than the officiating clergy can have significant involvement in the wedding. Special friends or members of the family may offer readings, meditations or prayers. Such participation should be invited well in advance of the wedding, and these parts should be consistent with the rest of the service. It would be good to know in advance exactly what will be spoken.

The sealing of the covenant with a kiss is not strictly part of most wedding services. It is, however, often added following the blessing or benediction. Occasionally, couples prefer not to include this kiss. They should be sure to let the presiding minister know their wishes.

This collection of wedding service resources is a beginning, not an end. If you have other materials, including your own words, which you believe will enrich your wedding service, let them be discussed with the person who officiates. One point is important here: This person should always be given the opportunity to express reservations if he or she believes that the inclusion of particular materials will compromise the integrity of the service or detract from the significance of the event.

If material from outside sources is used, it is the responsibility of the couple to have the material copied and given to the minister or priest in a form which allows it to be conveniently inserted in the service that he or she is reading from. If the loose-leaf version of this book is being used by the minister, additional materials should be prepared on punched, loose-leaf paper of the same size. This would greatly aid the person officiating.

An additional use of this book is that couples can have a record of their wedding service. This can be accomplished by recording the pages of the various selections on a three- by five-inch card or inside the front cover of this book. When friends ask for information about your wedding service, if you show them this book they will then have all the information available to them including the range of materials from which you have chosen your particular selections.

Part II
The Service

Orders of Worship

Choosing the order of worship, the sequence of the service, is the fundamental decision in planning a wedding. The choice, from the models presented here or developed from alternatives, determines the flow and spirit of the ceremony. The service may be brief, containing no more than the absolutely essential ingredients, or it may be enriched and lengthened with selections of music, scripture or other artistic expressions. Decisions should be carefully made in light of the couple's understanding of the meaning of the marriage relationship.

Most Protestant wedding ceremonies are quite brief — compared with the traditional Roman Catholic and Orthodox practice. The traditional Protestant service can be completed in about fifteen minutes. But the couple and their friends who have accepted the invitation to share the wedding ceremony are usually willing — if not eager — to participate in a more substantial celebration.

TRADITIONAL SERVICE

Processional
Opening Statement
Charge to the Couple
Questions of Willingness
Presentation of the Bride
Exchange of Vows
Blessing and Presentation of Ring or Rings
Declaration of Marriage
Wedding Prayer
The Lord's Prayer
Benediction
Recessional

UNITED CHURCH OF CHRIST

Processional Hymn
Call to Worship and Statement of Purpose
Opening Prayer
Declaration of Consent
Presentation of the Bride
Scripture Lessons
Sermon
Statement of Faith (Apostles' Creed or Other)
Covenant
Blessing and Presentation of Ring or Rings
Pronouncement of Marriage
Blessings and Wedding Prayers
The Lord's Prayer
Benediction

UNITED METHODIST CHURCH

GATHERING

Entrance
Greeting and Statement of Purpose
Question of Willingness
Affirmation of the Community

MINISTRY OF THE WORD

Opening Prayer
Reading or Readings from Scripture
Hymn or Other Music
Sermon
Intercessory Prayer

THE MARRIAGE

Exchange of Vows
Blessing and Presentation of the Ring or Rings
Announcement of Marriage
Doxology or Hymn

THANKSGIVING

[Option A]
  Prayer of Thanksgiving
  The Lord's Prayer
  Hymn or Psalm
[Option B]
  Holy Communion
    Offering of Ourselves
    Presentation of the Elements

Prayer of Thanksgiving
Sanctus (Holy, Holy, Holy)
Prayer of Consecration
The Lord's Prayer
Serving the Bread and Wine

[Option C]
Agape Meal
Offering for the Needy and Hungry
Scripture Readings
Testimonies
Extemporaneous Prayer
The Lord's Prayer
Passing of the Bread
Passing of the Cup

DISMISSAL WITH BLESSING AND THE PEACE

The Blessing
The Peace

AMERICAN LUTHERAN CHURCH

Greeting
Invocation
Scripture Lesson
Address
Hymn
Statement of Purpose
Question of Intention
Promises of Faithfulness
Exchange of Ring or Rings
Announcement of Marriage
Affirmation of Community
Wedding Prayers
Holy Communion and the Peace (Optional)
The Lord's Prayer
Benediction

EPISCOPAL CHURCH

Entrance
Address to the Congregation
Charge to the Couple
Declaration of Consent
Affirmation of the Community
Hymn, Psalm or Anthem

MINISTRY OF THE WORD

Opening Prayer
Holy Scripture
Homily or Other Response

THE MARRIAGE

Exchange of Vows
Blessing and Presentation of Ring or Rings
Pronouncement

THE PRAYERS

The Lord's Prayer
Intercessory Prayers

THE BLESSING OF THE MARRIAGE

Prayer of Thanksgiving
Benediction
The Peace
Holy Communion (Optional)
Recession or Hymn

UNITED CHURCH OF CANADA

Processional Hymn
Statement of Purpose
Prayer of Approach (Opening Prayer)
Lessons (Scripture)
Address to the People
Address (Charge) to the Couple and Legal Admonition
Questions (of Intent)
Presentation of the Bride
Prayer for Sincerity
Vows
Exchange of Ring or Rings
Declaration
Blessing
Prayer
The Lord's Prayer
Blessing

BRIEF CONTEMPORARY SERVICE

Greeting
Questions of Intent
Exchange of Vows
Exchange of Symbols (Rings)
Pronouncement of Marriage
Prayer
Blessing

LONGER CONTEMPORARY SERVICE

Calling the People Together
A Hymn or Other Special Music
A Gathering Prayer
Scripture or Other Readings
Statements of Willingness
Meditation, Sermon or Reflections
Presentation of the Bride
Exchange of Vows
Exchange of Rings or Tokens
Announcement of Marriage
A Prayer
A Hymn or Other Special Music
The Blessing and Sending Forth

4

Gathering Words

Whenever people come together for a formal occasion some words are needed to call the meeting to order. Those for a wedding suggest, or may in fact be, a call to worship — for in each tradition represented in this book the wedding ceremony is understood to be an expression of the worship of God.

Opening words state the purpose of the gathering. They can do this in language ranging from simple and direct to ornate and poetic. They acknowledge the importance of the event taking place, introduce the principal people in the gathering — the couple and the witnesses — and invite the community to be attentive to the moment.

The officiating person should speak them clearly and direct them to the entire company. While they are formal in that they open the observance of a rite, these words should also be warm in tone and inviting in spirit.

Sometimes it is well for the minister to offer the gathering words while the assembly remains standing, then, at the close, to invite the congregation to be seated. This provides for a transition from words addressed to the gathered community to words addressed to the couple.

Dearly beloved, we are gathered together here in the sight of God, and the presence of these witnesses, to join together this man and this woman in holy matrimony; which is an honorable estate, instituted of God, and signifying unto us the mystical union which exists between Christ and his Church; which holy estate Christ adorned and beautified with his presence in Cana of Galilee. It is therefore not to be entered into unadvisedly, but reverently, discreetly, and in the fear of God. Into this holy estate these two persons come now to be joined. If anyone can show just cause why they may not lawfully be joined together, let them now speak, or else hereafter forever hold their peace.

Traditional Service

In the name of the Father, and of the Son, and of the Holy Spirit. *Amen.*

or

Our help is in the name of the Lord who made heaven and earth. *Amen.*

Dearly Beloved, we are gathered together in the sight of God to join this man and this woman in marriage. Let all who enter it know that marriage is a sacred and joyous covenant, a way of life ordained of God from the beginning of his creation. "For this reason," says our Lord, "a man shall leave his father and mother and be joined to his wife, and the two shall become one flesh. What therefore God has joined together, let no man put asunder." Marriage is also compared by the apostle Paul to the mystical union between Christ and his church. Therefore, it should not be entered into unadvisedly or lightly, but reverently, considering the purposes for which it was ordained.

God has ordered the covenant of marriage: that husband and wife may give to each other companionship, help, and comfort, both in prosperity and in adversity; that he may hallow the expression of the natural affections; that children may be born and nurtured in families and trained in godliness; and that human society may stand on firm foundations.

Into this sacred covenant these two persons now desire to enter. Let us therefore invoke the blessing of God on the union now to be formed.

United Church of Christ

Friends, we are gathered as the Church to celebrate and praise God for the union of _____ and _____ in marriage. The bond and union of marriage were ordained by God, who created us male and female for each other. The Apostle Paul announced that where Christ is present, there is surely equality as well as unity. With his presence and power, Jesus graced a wedding at Cana of Galilee. _____ and _____ have come here to join in marriage.

United Methodist

GATHERING WORDS

Clergy: The grace of our Lord Jesus Christ, the love of God, and the communion of the Holy Spirit be with you all.

People: And also with you.

(The American Lutheran service provides here the Opening Prayer, Scripture, Address and Hymn.)

Clergy: The Lord God in his goodness created us male and female, and by the gift of marriage founded human community in a joy that begins now and is brought to perfection in the life to come.

Because of sin, our age-old rebellion, the gladness of marriage can be overcast and the gift of the family can become a burden.

But because God, who established marriage, continues still to bless it with his abundant and ever-present support, we can be sustained in our weariness and have our joy restored.

American Lutheran

Dearly beloved: We have come together in the presence of God to witness and bless the joining together of this man and this woman in Holy Matrimony. The bond and covenant of marriage was established by God in creation, and our Lord Jesus Christ adorned this manner of life by his presence and first miracle at a wedding in Cana of Galilee. It signifies to us the mystery of the union between Christ and his Church, and Holy Scripture commends it to be honored among all people.

The union of husband and wife in heart, body, and mind is intended by God for their mutual joy; for the help and comfort given one another in prosperity and adversity; and, when it is God's will, for the procreation of children and their nurture in the knowledge and love of the Lord. Therefore marriage is not to be entered into unadvisedly or lightly, but reverently, deliberately, and in accordance with the purposes for which it was instituted by God.

Into this holy union _____ and _____ now come to be joined. If any of you can show just cause why they may not lawfully be married, speak now; or else for ever hold your peace.

Episcopal

GATHERING WORDS

We, as a community of friends, are gathered here in God's presence, to witness the marriage of (Christian name and surname) and (Christian name and surname), and to ask God to bless them.

(The United Church of Canada service provides here the Opening Prayer and Scripture Lessons.)

By our presence here we accept responsibility for helping (Christian name) and (Christian name) and encouraging them in the new relationship into which they are about to enter.

Marriage, like our creation as men and women, owes its very existence to God. It is God's will and intention that a husband and wife should love each other throughout their life; (and that children born to them should enjoy the security of family and home).

United Church of Canada

Greetings in the name of the Father, Son and Holy Spirit. I welcome you to this special event in which _____ and _____ declare before you and God that they choose each other. It is an occasion which is both solemn, as we reflect on the seriousness of their decision, and festive, as we share their joy. We are witnessing an important event in the lives of these two friends.

Our service is based on the relationship which _____ and _____ share, and on their faith in God. It is a covenant. We affirm their love for each other as part of God's will for them.

Contemporary Service

We have come together — families and friends — in the presence of God to uphold _____ and _____ as they make their vows of marriage. We celebrate with them the love they have discovered in each other, and we support their decision to commit themselves to one another for the rest of their lives.

Marriage is a holy estate born in the love of God. It is a relationship entered into thoughtfully, reverently, with gratitude for the past and hope for the future. In the tradition of our faith, we believe God calls a man and a woman to leave the homes of their childhood to become, together, a new family.

Contemporary Service

5

Opening Prayers (Invocation)

An opening prayer or invocation is a reminder to all who participate in a service that this worship assumes the presence of God. While the traditional service does not have an opening prayer, it should be noted that most contemporary services do provide for prayer early in the worship.

Prayer always has an effect on the one who prays. It enables something mysterious to happen. The few moments spent in prayer at this point in the worship help set a mood for the remainder of the service.

Let us pray.

Almighty and most merciful Father, we your unworthy Children praise you for all the bounties of your providence, and for all the gifts of your grace. We thank you especially for the institution of marriage, which you have ordained to guard, to hallow, and to perfect the gift of love. We thank you for the joy which these your servants find in each other, and for the love and trust in which they enter this holy covenant. And since without your help we cannot do anything as we ought, we pray you to enrich your servants with your grace, that they may enter into their marriage as in your sight, and truly keep their vows; through Jesus Christ our Lord. *Amen.*

United Church of Christ

Clergy: The Lord be with you.

People: And also with you.

Clergy: Let us pray.

God of all peoples, we rejoice in your life in the midst of our lives. You are the true light illumining everyone. You show us the way, the truth, and the life. You love us even when we are unfaithful. You sustain us with your Holy Spirit. We praise you for your presence with us, and especially in this act of solemn covenant. Through Jesus Christ our Lord. *Amen.*

United Methodist

Let us pray.

Eternal God, our creator and redeemer, as you gladdened the wedding in Cana of Galilee by the presence of your Son, so by his presence now bring your joy to this wedding. Look in favor upon _____ and _____ and grant that they, rejoicing in all your gifts, may at length celebrate with Christ the marriage feast which has no end.

Amen.

American Lutheran

Clergy: The Lord be with you.

People: And also with you.

Let us pray.

O gracious and everliving God, you have created us male and female in your image: Look mercifully upon this man and this woman who come to you seeking your blessing, and assist them with your grace, that with true fidelity and steadfast love they may honor and keep the promises and vows they make; through Jesus Christ our Savior, who lives and reigns with you in the unity of the Holy Spirit, one God, for ever and ever.

Amen.   *Episcopal*

O God, you are the creator of all things; you made us, and
   you sustain us; we depend on you.
For the gift of life, we praise you.
For being able to think about its meaning and purpose, we
   thank you.
In the world without, and in our lives within, there is much
   that is confusing and contradictory.
Many voices counsel us; many forces pressure us; many
   things tempt us.
We need your light to lead us, your hand to hold us, and your
   love to complete us.
In Jesus' name we ask for your blessing now.
   Amen.

United Church of Canada

Let us pray.

We do not seek your presence, but rather we acknowledge it, God. You have declared in Jesus that you are present when we gather together. We affirm that you are among us. Help us to be conscious of your activity as we worship. Let your special blessing be upon _____ and _____ as they renew their covenant with you and declare their covenant with one another. We seek to be blessed in the name of Jesus, the Christ. *Amen.*

Contemporary Service

Eternal God, whom in Jesus Christ we have learned to call Father, we give thanks to you for the gift of life, and for its renewal with each day. We gather as in the presence of a loving Parent to celebrate this time which brings _____ and _____ to the threshold of their marriage.

For the dreams they have dreamed, and for their hopes for themselves and for each other we give thanks. We pray that the words and spirit of our gathering may be filled with meaning which will deepen with the passing years, through Jesus Christ our Lord. *Amen.*

Contemporary Service

6

Charge to the Couple

The charge to the couple is a reminder to the couple and others present that the wedding commitment is among the most serious of all decisions. It must not be taken lightly or without reflection on all implications involved. The couple is asked to declare before God, one another and those assembled that they recognize the importance of their pledge and are committed to honor it for the rest of their lives.

I require and charge you both, as you stand in the presence of God, before whom the secrets of all hearts are disclosed, that, having duly considered the holy covenant you are about to make, you do now declare before this company, your pledge of faith, each to the other. Be well assured that if these solemn vows be kept inviolate, as God's Word demands, and if steadfastly you endeavor to do the will of your heavenly Father, God will bless your marriage, will grant you fulfillment in it, and will establish your home in peace.

Traditional Service

I require and charge you both, here in the presence of God, that if either of you know any reason why you may not be united in marriage lawfully, and in accordance with God's Word, you do now confess it.

Episcopal

(Christian name and Christian name), your marriage is intended to join you for life in a relationship so intimate and personal that it will change your whole being.

It offers you the hope, and indeed the promise, of a love that is true and mature.

To attain such love you will have to commit yourselves to each other freely and gladly for the sake of a richer and deeper life together.

Let God be your guide and helper.

(Christian name and surname) and (Christian name and surname) you have made it known that you want to be joined in Christian marriage, and no one has shown any valid reason why you may not.

If either of you know any lawful impediment why you should not be married you are now to declare it.

United Church of Canada

_____ and _____, I call to your attention the seriousness of the decision which you have made and the covenant you are about to declare before God and these guests. Be very clear that your marriage is dependent upon your willingness to be faithful to each other and faithful to your understanding of God's will for you. Unfaithfulness in either is a betrayal of your covenant. Constant and continuous obedience to your vow will result in a marriage which will be blessed, a home which will be a place of peace, and a relationship in which you both grow in love.

Contemporary Service

_____ and _____, I remind you, as you stand in the presence of God, that love and loyalty are the foundation of a happy and enduring home.

During the days of your engagement you have given careful thought to the meaning of your marriage. You began the joining of your lives — and we pray that you will continue to grow together throughout the time you share.

The future is unknown to any of us. Yet your love for one another and trust in the goodness of God's will make possible the act of faith you now make in our midst.

As you exchange your vows of faithfulness, we will be listening and supporting you with our love. As you make your promises to each other, we will be reminded of promises we have made and be moved to renew our own.

Contemporary Service

Declaration
of Consent

An agreement to marry, as in every other legal contract, requires for its validity the consent of parties who offer their commitment freely, willingly and without coercion. From ancient times the freedom of each party has been held to be of importance. Before the vows are exchanged and — in the traditional arrangements — while the bride is still within the protection of her family, as symbolized by the father or other family representative who may stand at this point between the bride and groom, the question of willingness to offer the vows is asked: "Will you have this person...?"

The words of the declaration of consent are similar, as they must be, to the vows themselves. They serve as a preparation for the vows, and in their responses the bride and groom are saying to the gathered community: "It is my intention to uphold the integrity of my word by offering my commitment to this person who has chosen me and whom I have chosen."

DECLARATION OF CONSENT

_____ , will you have this woman to be your wedded wife, to live together in the holy estate of matrimony? Will you love her, comfort her, honor and keep her in sickness and in health, and, forsaking all others, keep you only unto her, so long as you both shall live?

Answer: I will.

_____ , will you have this man to be your wedded husband, to live together in the holy estate of matrimony? Will you love him, comfort him, honor and keep him in sickness and in health, and forsaking all others, keep you only unto him, so long as you both shall live?

Answer: I will.

Traditional Service

_____, will you have this woman to be your wife, and be faithful to her alone?

Answer: I will, with the help of God.

_____, will you have this man to be your husband, and be faithful to him alone?

Answer: I will, with the help of God.

United Church of Christ

DECLARATION OF CONSENT

_____ and _____ , if it is your intention to share with each other your joys and sorrows and all that the years will bring, with your promises bind yourselves to each other as husband and wife.

American Lutheran

Christ calls you into union with him and with one another. I ask you now in the presence of God and this congregation to declare your intent.

Will you have this man to be your husband, to live together in a holy marriage? Will you love him, comfort him, honor and keep him in sickness and in health, and forsaking all other, be faithful to him as long as you both shall live?

Answer: I will.

Will you have this woman to be your wife, to live together in a holy marriage? Will you love her, comfort her, honor and keep her in sickness and in health, and forsaking all other, be faithful to her as long as you both shall live?

Answer: I will.

United Methodist

DECLARATION OF CONSENT

_____, will you have this man to be your husband; to live together in the covenant of marriage? Will you love him, comfort him, honor and keep him, in sickness and in health; and, forsaking all others, be faithful to him as long as you both shall live?

Answer: I will.

_____, will you have this woman to be your wife; to live together in the covenant of marriage? Will you love her, comfort her, honor and keep her, in sickness and in health; and, forsaking all others, be faithful to her as long as you both shall live?

Answer: I will.

Episcopal

(Christian name), will you have this woman to be your wife?

Answer: I will.

(Christian name), will you have this man to be your husband?

Answer: I will.

                                            United Church of Canada

DECLARATION OF CONSENT

(Man's Christian name), do you here in the presence of God and these witnesses declare your commitment to (woman's Christian name) and choose her as the one with whom you wish to spend your life? Do you give yourself to her and accept the gift of self which she gives to you? Do you pledge to endure all of the difficulties which life may offer, even as you look forward to sharing the joys to be experienced together?

Answer: I do.

(Woman's Christian name), do you here in the presence of God and these witnesses declare your commitment to (man's Christian name) and choose him as the one with whom you wish to spend your life? Do you give yourself to him and accept the gift of self which he gives to you? Do you pledge to endure all of the difficulties which life may offer, even as you look forward to sharing the joys to be experienced together?

Answer: I do.

Contemporary Service

The covenant of marriage is one that can be entered into only by persons who are both legally and spiritually free to offer themselves to one another.

(Man's Christian name), do you come of your free will and with a conscious desire to be united in marriage with (woman's Christian name)?

Answer: I do.

Will you promise to care for (woman's Christian name) in the joys and sorrows of life, come what may, and to share the responsibility for growth and enrichment of your life together?

Answer: I will.

(Woman's Christian name), do you come of your free will and with a conscious desire to be united in marriage with (man's Christian name)?

Answer: I do.

Will you promise to care for (man's Christian name) in the joys and sorrows of life, come what may, and to share the responsibility for growth and enrichment of your life together?

Answer: I will.

Contemporary Service

Presentation
of the Bride

The presentation of the bride represents a tradition which called for the families to release their children for marriage. More particularly, fathers had responsibility for "giving" their daughters to men who were seen to be appropriate as mates. While this tradition may carry some of the now-unacceptable content of women as property, it has value for many people still in that it provides an opportunity for the family to offer its support and affirmation as a wedding takes place.

Here the term "presentation of the bride" is used, but alternatives, as it will be seen, may involve families of both the bride and groom offering support and affirmation. This dual emphasis has also been reflected in weddings where couples have chosen to include the groom and best man in the procession rather than to have the bride brought to the groom.

Clergy: Who gives this woman to be married to this man?

The Person Who Gives the Woman: I do.   *or*   Her mother and I do.

Traditional Service

Clergy: Who gives this woman to be married to this man?
The Person Who Gives the Woman: I do.

United Church of Christ

Clergy: Will all of you witnessing these promises do all in your power to uphold these two persons in their marriage?

People: We will.

Clergy: Who gives this woman to be married to this man?

The Father or a Friend: I do.

Episcopal

PRESENTATION OF THE BRIDE

Clergy: Who gives this woman to be married to this man?

Answer: I do.

United Church of Canada

Clergy: Who stands with this woman to symbolize the traditions and family out of which she comes?

The Father, Both Parents, Entire Family or Friend (standing in place): I do. *or* We do.

Clergy: Who stands with this man to symbolize the traditions and family out of which he comes?

The Father, Both Parents, Entire Family or Friend (standing in place): I do. *or* We do.

Contemporary Service

(The clergyman or -woman invites parents or family representatives to stand behind the bride and groom.)

Clergy: The union of _____ and _____ brings together two family traditions, two systems of roots, in the hope that a new family tree may become strong and fruitful. Theirs is a personal choice and a decision for which they are primarily responsible. Yet their life will be enriched by the support of the families from which each comes.

Clergy: Will you (parents or family representatives) encourage _____ and _____ in their marriage?

Answer: We will.

Clergy: Do you celebrate with them the decision they have made to choose each other?

Answer: We do.

Clergy: Will you continue to stand beside them, yet not between?

Answer: We will.

Contemporary Service

9

Scripture Lessons (Bible Readings)

While the coming together of a man and a woman in marriage is older than the Bible, biblical materials influence our concept of marriage and the wedding service. Many couples choose to include an appropriate passage or passages of scripture in an effort to express their spiritual heritage and to turn the service to words which address us as the human family.

The suggestions made by the several denominations represented in this book are too numerous to reprint. We have chosen from among those offerings. You are encouraged to read all the selections and choose the readings which will be most appropriate for your wedding. Of course, many other selections are possible from the Bible.

Several services call for three scripture readings: Old Testament, Epistle and Gospel. We recommend this to you. However, we realize that some couples may prefer to include one Old Testament and one New Testament reading (rather than three readings), and other couples may prefer a single lesson from the Bible. Make the choices which will have meaning for you.

Then God said, "Let us make man in our image, after our likeness; and let them have dominion over the fish of the sea, and over the birds of the air, and over the cattle, and over all the earth, and over every creeping thing that creeps upon the earth." So God created man in his own image, in the image of God he created him; male and female he created them. And God blessed them, and God said to them, "Be fruitful and multiply, and fill the earth and subdue it; and have dominion over the fish of the sea and over the birds of the air and over every living thing that moves upon the earth." And God said, "Behold, I have given you every plant yielding seed which is upon the face of all the earth, and every tree with seed in its fruit; you shall have them for food. And to every beast of the earth, and to every bird of the air, and to everything that creeps on the earth, everything that has the breath of life, I have given every green plant for food." And it was so. And God saw everything that he had made, and behold, it was very good. And there was evening and there was morning, a sixth day.

Genesis 1:26 - 31

Then the Lord God said, "It is not good that the man should be alone; I will make him a helper fit for him." So out of the ground the Lord God formed every beast of the field and every bird of the air, and brought them to the man, to see what he would call them; and whatever the man called every living creature, that was its name. The man gave names to all cattle, and to the birds of the air, and to every beast of the field; but for the man there was not found a helper fit for him. So the Lord God caused a deep sleep to fall upon the man, and while he slept took one of his ribs and closed up its place with flesh; and the rib which the Lord God had taken from the man he made into a woman and brought her to the man. Then the man said, "This at last is bone of my bones and flesh of my flesh; she shall be called Woman, because she was taken out of Man." Therefore a man leaves his father and his mother and cleaves to his wife, and they become one flesh. And the man and his wife were both naked and were not ashamed.

Genesis 2:18 - 25

To the choirmaster; with stringed instruments.
A Psalm. A Song.

May God be gracious to us and bless us and make his face to shine upon us, that thy way may be known upon earth, thy saving power among all nations. Let the peoples praise thee, O God; let all the peoples praise thee!

Let the nations be glad and sing for joy, for thou dost judge the peoples with equity and guide the nations upon earth. Let the peoples praise thee, O God; let all the peoples praise thee!

The earth has yielded its increase; God, our God, has blessed us. God has blessed us; let all the ends of the earth fear him!

Psalm 67

Unless the Lord builds the house, those who build it labor in vain. Unless the Lord watches over the city, the watchman stays awake in vain. It is in vain that you rise up early and go late to rest, eating the bread of anxious toil; for he gives to his beloved in sleep.

Lo, sons are a heritage from the Lord, the fruit of the womb a reward. Like arrows in the hand of a warrior are the sons of one's youth. Happy is the man who has his quiver full of them! He shall not be put to shame when he speaks with his enemies in the gate.

Psalm 127

Come, bless the Lord, all you servants of the Lord, who stand by night in the house of the Lord! Lift up your hands to the holy place, and bless the Lord!

May the Lord bless you from Zion, he who made heaven and earth!

Psalm 134

Behold, the days are coming, says the Lord, when I will make a new covenant with the house of Israel and the house of Judah, not like the covenant which I made with their fathers when I took them by the hand to bring them out of the land of Egypt, my covenant which they broke, though I was their husband, says the Lord. But this is the covenant which I will make with the house of Israel after those days, says the Lord; I will put my law within them, and I will write it upon their hearts; and I will be their God, and they shall be my people. And no longer shall each man teach his neighbor and each his brother, saying, 'Know the Lord,' for they shall all know me, from the least of them to the greatest, says the Lord, for I will forgive their iniquity, and I will remember their sin no more.

Jeremiah 31:31 - 34

I appeal to you therefore, brethren, by the mercies of God, to present your bodies as a living sacrifice, holy and acceptable to God, which is your spiritual worship. Do not be conformed to this world but be transformed by the renewal of your mind, that you may prove what is the will of God, what is good and acceptable and perfect. For by the grace given to me I bid every one among you not to think of himself more highly than he ought to think, but to think with sober judgment, each according to the measure of faith which God has assigned him.

Let love be genuine; hate what is evil, hold fast to what is good; love one another with brotherly affection; outdo one another in showing honor. Never flag in zeal, be aglow with the Spirit, serve the Lord. Rejoice in your hope, be patient in tribulation, be constant in prayer. Contribute to the needs of the saints, practice hospitality.

Romans 12:1 - 3, 9 - 13

Love is patient and kind; love is not jealous or boastful; it is not arrogant or rude. Love does not insist on its own way; it is not irritable or resentful; it does not rejoice at wrong, but rejoices in the right. Love bears all things, believes all things, hopes all things, endures all things. Love never ends.

1 Corinthians 13:4 - 8a

For this reason I bow my knees before the Father, from whom every family in heaven and on earth is named, that according to the riches of his glory he may grant you to be strengthened with might through his Spirit in the inner man, and that Christ may dwell in your hearts through faith; that you, being rooted and grounded in love, may have power to comprehend with all the saints what is the breadth and length and height and depth, and to know the love of Christ which surpasses knowledge, that you may be filled with all the fullness of God.

Now to him who by the power at work within us is able to do far more abundantly than all that we ask or think, to him be glory in the church and in Christ Jesus to all generations, for ever and ever. Amen.

Ephesians 3:14 - 21

Put on then, as God's chosen ones, holy and beloved, compassion, kindness, lowliness, meekness, and patience, forbearing one another and, if one has a complaint against another, forgiving each other; as the Lord has forgiven you, so you also must forgive. And above all these put on love, which binds everything together in perfect harmony. And let the peace of Christ rule in your hearts, to which indeed you were called in the one body. And be thankful. Let the word of Christ dwell in you richly, as you teach and admonish one another in all wisdom, and as you sing psalms and hymns and spiritual songs with thankfulness in your hearts to God. And whatever you do, in word or deed, do everything in the name of the Lord Jesus, giving thanks to God the Father through him.

Colossians 3:12 - 17

Little children, let us not love in word or speech but in deed and in truth.

By this we shall know that we are of the truth, and reassure our hearts before him whenever our hearts condemn us, for God is greater than our hearts, and he knows everything. Beloved, if our hearts do not condemn us, we have confidence before God; and we receive from him whatever we ask, because we keep his commandments and do what pleases him. And this is his commandment, that we should believe in the name of his Son Jesus Christ and love one another, just as he has commanded us. All who keep his commandments abide in him, and he in them. And by this we know that he abides in us, by the Spirit which he has given us.

1 John 3:18 - 24

Beloved, let us love one another; for love is of God, and he who loves is born of God and knows God. He who does not love does not know God; for God is love. In this the love of God was made manifest among us, that God sent his only Son into the world, so that we might live through him. In this is love, not that we loved God but that he loved us and sent his Son to be the expiation for our sins. Beloved, if God so loved us, we also ought to love one another. No man has ever seen God; if we love one another, God abides in us and his love is perfected in us.

1 John 4:7 - 12

And he opened his mouth and taught them, saying:

"Blessed are the poor in spirit, for theirs is the kingdom of heaven.

"Blessed are those who mourn, for they shall be comforted.

"Blessed are the meek, for they shall inherit the earth.

"Blessed are those who hunger and thirst for righteousness, for they shall be satisfied.

"Blessed are the merciful, for they shall obtain mercy.

"Blessed are the pure in heart, for they shall see God.

"Blessed are the peacemakers, for they shall be called sons of God."

Matthew 5:2 - 4

"Not every one who says to me, 'Lord, Lord,' shall enter the kingdom of heaven, but he who does the will of my Father who is in heaven.

"Every one then who hears these words of mine and does them will be like a wise man who built his house upon the rock; and the rain fell, and the floods came, and the winds blew and beat upon that house, but it did not fall, because it had been founded on the rock. And every one who hears these words of mine and does not do them will be like a foolish man who built his house upon the sand; and the rain fell, and the floods came, and the winds blew and beat against that house, and it fell; and great was the fall of it."

And when Jesus finished these sayings, the crowds were astonished at his teaching, for he taught them as one who had authority, and not as their scribes.

Matthew 7:21, 24 - 29

He answered, "Have you not read that he who made them from the beginning made them male and female, and said, 'For this reason a man shall leave his father and mother and be joined to his wife, and the two shall become one'? So they are no longer two but one. What therefore God has joined together, let no man put asunder."

Matthew 19:4 - 6

And one of them, a lawyer, asked him a question, to test him. "Teacher, which is the great commandment in the law?" And he said to him, "You shall love the Lord your God with all your heart, and with all your soul, and with all your mind. This is the great and first commandment. And a second is like it, You shall love your neighbor as yourself. On these two commandments depend all the law and the prophets."

Matthew 22:35 - 40

On the third day there was a marriage in Cana in Galilee, and the mother of Jesus was there; Jesus also was invited to the marriage, with his disciples. When the wine failed, the mother of Jesus said to him, "They have no wine." And Jesus said to her, "O woman, what have you to do with me? My hour has not yet come." His mother said to the servants, "Do whatever he tells you." Now six stone jars were standing there, for the Jewish rites of purification, each holding twenty or thirty gallons. Jesus said to them, "Fill the jars with water." And they filled them up to the brim. He said to them, "Now draw some out, and take it to the steward of the feast." So they took it. When the steward of the feast tasted the water now become wine, and did not know where it came from (though the servants who had drawn the water knew), the steward of the feast called the bridegroom and said to him, "Every man serves the good wine first; and when men have drunk freely, then the poor wine; but you have kept the good wine until now." This, the first of his signs, Jesus did at Cana in Galilee, and manifested his glory; and his disciples believed in him.

John 2:1 - 11

"These things I have spoken to you, that my joy may be in you, and that your joy may be full.

"This is my commandment, that you love one another as I have loved you. Greater love has no man than this, that a man lay down his life for his friends. You are my friends if you do what I command you. No longer do I call you servants, for the servant does not know what his master is doing; but I have called you friends, for all that I have heard from my Father I have made known to you. You did not choose me, but I chose you and appointed you that you should go and bear fruit and that your fruit should abide; so that whatever you ask the Father in my name, he may give it to you. This I command you, to love one another."

John 15:11 - 17

10

The Exchange of Vows

An absolute requirement in a wedding is the agreement of a couple in the presence of official witnesses to take one another as husband and wife. The exchange of vows represents the moment of covenant. The words which express the act of commitment are often considered to be the most significant in the ceremony. They are those which express: "I choose you. I accept your having chosen me. I commit myself to you." The vows may also include mutual hopes for and commitment to happiness together and an understanding that the commitment will be secure as it is tested through periods of sadness, times of difficulty and seasons of disappointment. It is always a covenant "for better or for worse."

After carefully studying the wordings of the vows in the ceremonies offered here — and perhaps selecting one from among them — it may be that the couple will wish to translate the spirit of these expressions into a language that more nearly reflects their own understanding. They also may have additional thoughts to share with one another. In recent years there has been increasing interest among couples and the clergy for creative expression in the vows. If there is a departure from the traditional wordings of the vows, one must make especially certain that the spirit of the commitment to a lifetime of faithfulness is clearly maintained.

I, _____, take thee, _____, to be my wedded wife, to have and to hold, from this day forward, for better, for worse, for richer, for poorer, in sickness and in health, to love and to cherish, till death us do part, according to God's holy ordinance; and thereto I pledge thee my faith.

I, _____, take thee, _____, to be my wedded husband, to have and to hold, from this day forward, for better, for worse, for richer, for poorer, in sickness and in health, to love and to cherish, till death us do part, according to God's holy ordinance; and thereto I pledge thee my faith.

Traditional Service

I, _____, take you, _____, to be my wife, and I promise to love and sustain you in the bonds of marriage from this day forward, in sickness and in health, in plenty and in want, in joy and in sorrow, till death shall part us, according to God's holy ordinance.

I, _____, take you, _____, to be my husband, and I promise to love and sustain you in the bonds of marriage from this day forward, in sickness and in health, in plenty and in want, in joy and in sorrow, till death shall part us, according to God's holy ordinance.

United Church of Christ

In the name of God, I, _____, take you, _____, to be my wife, to have and to hold from this day forward, for better for worse, for richer for poorer, in sickness and in health, to love and to cherish, until we are parted by death. This is my solemn vow.

In the name of God, I, _____, take you, _____, to be my husband, to have and to hold from this day forward, for better for worse, for richer for poorer, in sickness and in health, to love and to cherish, until we are parted by death. This is my solemn vow.

United Methodist

I take you, _____, to be my wife from this day forward, to join with you and share all that is to come, and I promise to be faithful to you until death parts us.

I take you, _____, to be my husband from this day forward, to join with you and share all that is to come, and I promise to be faithful to you until death parts us.

American Lutheran

In the name of God, I, _____, take you, _____, to be my wife, to have and to hold from this day forward, for better for worse, for richer for poorer, in sickness and in health, to love and to cherish, until we are parted by death. This is my solemn vow.

In the name of God, I, _____, take you, _____, to be my husband, to have and to hold from this day forward, for better for worse, for richer for poorer, in sickness and in health, to love and to cherish, until we are parted by death. This is my solemn vow.

Episcopal

EXCHANGE OF VOWS

Prayer for Sincerity

Let us pray for this man and woman as they make their marriage vows.

Our Father, as _____ and _____ pledge themselves to each other, help them and bless them; that their love may be pure, and their vows may be true; through Jesus Christ our Lord. *Amen.*

Vows

Take (woman's Christian name) by the right hand and say to her: _____, I take you to be my wife;
  to laugh with you in joy;
  to grieve with you in sorrow;
  to grow with you in love;
  serving mankind in peace and hope;
  as long as we both shall live.

Take (man's Christian name) by the right hand and say to him: _____, I take you to be my husband;
  to laugh with you in joy;
  to grieve with you in sorrow;
  to grow with you in love;
  serving mankind in peace and hope;
  as long as we both shall live.

United Church of Canada

_____, I covenant with you to be your husband. I offer you my love and my support throughout all of our lives. I commit myself to years of growth and sharing as I encourage you to move in new directions. I will strive to achieve my potential as God's creature and will celebrate your progress toward the same goal. I give myself as I am and as I will be, and I do it for all of life.

_____, I covenant with you to be your wife. I offer you my love and my support throughout all of our lives. I commit myself to years of growth and sharing as I encourage you to move in new directions. I will strive to achieve my potential as God's creature and will celebrate your progress toward the same goal. I give myself as I am and as I will be, and I do it for all of life.

Contemporary Service

EXCHANGE OF VOWS

I, _____, promise you, _____, to be your husband as long as I live. I promise to love you and to support your growing toward full maturity. I promise to seek peace for ourselves, for our children, and for the world which encircles us. As I commit myself to care for you, I also offer myself into your loving care, now and throughout our lives.

I, _____, promise you, _____, to be your wife as long as I live. I promise to love you and to support your growing toward full maturity. I promise to seek peace for ourselves, for our children, and for the world which encircles us. As I commit myself to care for you, I also offer myself into your loving care, now and throughout our lives.

Contemporary Service

11

Blessing and Presentation of Rings

The wedding ring is the traditional symbol of the pledges exchanged on the wedding day. It is most often a plain band without stones or special engraving. The ring is a symbol of the promises binding two people together in a special relationship. It is the promises themselves which are important, but the ring, or token, is a physical reminder of ties which cannot be seen by the human eye. Like our relationship with God, which is often symbolized by sacraments or objects, relationships in marriage are far beyond the physical.

BLESSING AND PRESENTATION OF RINGS

Clergy: Let us pray.

Clergy: Bless, O Lord, the giving of these rings, that they who wear them may abide in thy peace, and continue in thy favor; through Jesus Christ our Lord. *Amen.*

Man: In token and pledge of our constant faith and abiding love, with this ring I thee wed, in the name of the Father, and of the Son, and of the Holy Spirit. *Amen.*

Woman: In token and pledge of our constant faith and abiding love, with this ring I thee wed, in the name of the Father, and of the Son, and of the Holy Spirit. *Amen.*

Traditional Service

Man: This ring I give you in token of my faithfulness and love, and as a pledge to honor you with my whole being, and to share with you my worldly goods.

Woman: This ring I give you in token of my faithfulness and love, and as a pledge to honor you with my whole being, and to share with you my worldly goods.

or

Man: I give you this ring in token of the covenant made today between us; in the name of the Father, and of the Son, and of the Holy Spirit.

Woman: I give you this ring in token of the covenant made today between us; in the name of the Father, and of the Son, and of the Holy Spirit.

United Church of Christ

Clergy: Bless, O Lord, the giving of these rings (symbols), that they who wear them may live in your peace, and continue in your favor all the days of their life, through Jesus Christ our Lord. *Amen.*

Man: _____, I give you this ring as a sign of my vow, and with all that I am, and all that I have, I honor you [in the name of the Father, and of the Son, and of the Holy Spirit].

Woman: _____, I give you this ring as a sign of my vow, and with all that I am, and all that I have, I honor you [in the name of the Father, and of the Son, and of the Holy Spirit].

United Methodist

Man: I give you this ring as a sign of my love and faithfulness.

Woman: I give you this ring as a sign of my love and faithfulness.

American Lutheran

Clergy: Bless, O Lord, *this ring* to be *a sign* of the vows by which this man and this woman have bound themselves to each other; through Jesus Christ our Lord. *Amen.*

Man: I give you this ring as a symbol of my vow, and with all that I am, and all that I have, I honor you, in the Name of the Father, and of the Son, and of the Holy Spirit (or in the Name of God).

Woman: I give you this ring as a symbol of my vow, and with all that I am, and all that I have, I honor you, in the Name of the Father, and of the Son, and of the Holy Spirit (or in the Name of God).

Episcopal

Man: _____, I give you this ring that you may wear it as a symbol of our marriage.

Woman: _____, I give you this ring that you may wear it as a symbol of our marriage.

United Church of Canada

BLESSING AND PRESENTATION OF RINGS

(The clergy receives the ring or rings, and holds one or both rings up before the congregation.)

Clergy: The circle has long been a symbol of God. Without beginning or end and with no point of weakness, the circle is a reminder of the eternal quality of God and of unending strength. Thus, this ring (these rings) serve(s) to remind us of the relationship which _____ and _____ have with God as well as the relationship which they have with one another. The rings are symbols of covenant and should serve as reminders of our need to be faithful in all our relationships.

Clergy: Let us pray for God's blessing upon those who give and receive this ring (these rings).

Clergy: Creator God, we seek a special blessing, upon _____ and _____ as they give and receive this ring (these rings). Let them be ever conscious of your love and faithfulness as they are faithful to one another. Bless them by their love for one another and by your presence in their new family. *Amen.*

Man: _____, I give you this ring as a symbol of my love for you, my covenant to be your husband and to be faithful to you, and as a reminder of God's presence in your life.

Woman: _____, I give you this ring as a symbol of my love for you, my covenant to be your wife and to be faithful to you, and as reminder of God's presence in your life.

Contemporary Service

Clergy: The vows which have been exchanged by
_____ and _____ have been offered in our
hearing. But words are fleeting, and the sound of them is
soon gone. Therefore, the wedding ring becomes an enduring symbol of the promises which have been made.

Clergy: May these wedding rings be a reminder to
_____ and _____ of the vows they have shared
today and a witness to all the world of their commitment
in marriage.

Man: As a symbol of my love for you and my commitment to you throughout our lives, I give you this ring, in
the name of the Father, and of the Son, and of the Holy
Spirit. *Amen.*

Woman: As a symbol of my love for you and my commitment to you throughout our lives, I give you this ring, in
the name of the Father, and of the Son, and of the Holy
Spirit. *Amen.*

Contemporary Service

12

Pronouncement
or Declaration

This is the moment when the person who is officiating says, "It is completed." The purpose for which the people have gathered has been realized and the act of covenant is now fulfilled. The word of declaration or pronouncement is the moment of climax in the wedding service.

This is also a significant moment as far as the law is concerned. The officiating person is obliged to marry the couple. This means that he or she, having discerned their willingness to be married and having heard their vows, must now declare by the power vested in him or her that they are married. The declaration or pronouncement is the exact moment of marriage.

Forasmuch as _____ and _____ have consented together in holy wedlock, and have witnessed the same before God and this company, and thereto have pledged their faith each to the other, and have declared the same by joining hands and by giving and receiving rings; I pronounce that they are husband and wife together, in the name of the Father, and of the Son, and of the Holy Spirit. Those whom God hath joined together, let no one put asunder. *Amen.*

Traditional Service

PRONOUNCEMENT OR DECLARATION

Forasmuch as you, _____ and _____ , have consented together in this sacred covenant, and have declared the same before God and this company, I pronounce you husband and wife, in the name of the Father, and of the Son, and of the Holy Spirit. *Amen.*

United Church of Christ

You have declared your consent and vows before God and this congregation. May God confirm your covenant, and fill you both with grace.

Now that _____ and _____ have given themselves to each other by solemn vows, with the joining of hands, and the giving of rings, I announce to you that they are husband and wife in the name of the Father, and of the Son, and of the Holy Spirit. Those whom God has joined together, let no one separate. *Amen.*

United Methodist

Clergy: _____ and _____, by their promises before God and in the presence of this congregation, have bound themselves to one another as husband and wife.

People: Blessed be the Father and the Son and the Holy Spirit now and forever.

Clergy: Those whom God has joined together let no one put asunder.

People: Amen.

Clergy: The Lord God, who created our first parents and established them in marriage, establish and sustain you, that you may find delight in each other and grow in holy love until your life's end.

People: Amen.

American Lutheran

Now that _____ and _____ have given themselves to each other by solemn vows, with the joining of hands and the giving and receiving of *a ring,* I pronounce that they are husband and wife, in the Name of the Father, and of the Son, and of the Holy Spirit.

Those whom God has joined together let no one put asunder. *Amen.*

Episcopal

Declaration

Forasmuch as _____ and _____ have made this solemn covenant of marriage before God and all of us here, I declare them to be husband and wife; in the name of God, Father, Son, and Holy Spirit. *Amen.*

Blessing

The grace of Christ attend you,
the love of God surround you,
the Holy Spirit keep you. *Amen.*

(The marriage vows may be sealed with a kiss.)

United Church of Canada

In consideration of the events which we have witnessed, including the exchange of covenant between _____ and _____ and their willingness to share life in faithfulness to one another and to God, I declare to you that they are husband and wife. Their marriage is blessed by God.

Contemporary Service

Because _____ and _____ have exchanged their promises of faithful love, and because in our presence they have exchanged symbols which make their covenant visible, therefore we now recognize before God and the community that _____ and _____ are husband and wife, in the name of God. *Amen.*

Contemporary Service

Wedding
Prayers

After the couple have exchanged their vows, after the completion of the wedding has been announced, it is time to thank God. The wedding prayer is a time for celebration and for the asking of God's blessing upon the new family. It always seems appropriate that the first act of a newly married couple is to pray to God and to ask for a blessing for their life together.

O eternal God, creator and preserver of all, giver of all spiritual grace, the author of everlasting life: Send thy blessing upon this man and this woman, whom we bless in thy name; that they may surely perform and keep the vow and covenant between them made, and may ever remain in perfect love and peace together, and live according to thy laws.

Look graciously upon them, that they may love, honor, and cherish each other, and so live together in faithfulness and patience, in wisdom and true godliness, that their home may be a haven of blessing and a place of peace; through Jesus Christ our Lord. *Amen.*

Traditional Service

God the Father, God the Son, and God the Holy Spirit bless, preserve, and keep you; the Lord mercifully with his favor look upon you, and fill you with all spiritual benediction and grace, that you may so live together in this life, that in the world to come you may have life everlasting. *Amen.*

Let us pray.

Almighty and most merciful God, having now united this man and woman in the holy covenant of marriage, grant them grace to live therein according to your holy word; strengthen them in constant faithfulness and true affection toward each other; sustain and defend them in all trials and temptations; and help them so to pass through this world in faith toward you, in communion with your church, and in loving service one of the other, that they may enjoy forever your heavenly benediction; through Jesus Christ our Lord. *Amen.*

United Church of Christ

WEDDING PRAYERS

Intercessory Prayer

Gracious God, bless this man and woman who come now to join in marriage, that they may give their vows to each other in the strength and spirit of your steadfast love. Let the promise of your word root and grow in their lives. Grant them vision and hope to persevere in trust and friendship all their days. Keep ever before them the needs of the world. By your grace enable them to be true disciples of Jesus Christ, in whose name we pray. *Amen.*

Prayer of Thanksgiving

Minister: Friends, let us give thanks to the Lord.

People: Thanks be to God.

Minister: Most gracious God, we give you thanks for your tender love in sending Jesus Christ to come among us, to be born of a human mother, and to make the way of the cross to be the way of life. We thank you, also, for consecrating the union of man and woman in his Name. By the power of your Holy Spirit, pour out the abundance of your blessing upon this man and woman in his Name. Defend them from every enemy. Lead them into all peace. Let their love for each other be a seal upon their hearts, a mantle about their shoulders, and a crown upon their foreheads. Bless them in their work and in their companionship; in their sleeping and in their waking; in their joys and in their sorrows; in their life and in their death. Finally, in your mercy bring them to that table where your saints feast for ever in your heavenly home; through Jesus Christ our Lord, who with you and the Holy Spirit lives and reigns, one God, for ever and ever. *Amen.*

United Methodist

Let us bless God for all the gifts in which we rejoice today.

Lord God, constant in mercy, great in faithfulness: With high praise we recall your acts of unfailing love for the human family, for the house of Israel, and for your people the Church.

We bless you for the joy which your servants, _____ and _____, have found in each other, and pray that you give to us such a sense of your constant love that we may employ all our strength in a life of praise of you, whose work alone holds true and endures forever. *Amen.*

Let us pray for _____ and _____ in their life together.

Faithful Lord, source of love, pour down your grace upon _____ and _____, that they may fulfill the vows they have made this day and reflect your steadfast love in their life-long faithfulness to each other. As members with them of the body of Christ, use us to support their life together; and from your great store of strength give them power and patience, affection and understanding, courage, and love toward you, toward each other, and toward the world, that they may continue together in mutual growth according to your will in Jesus Christ our Lord. *Amen.*

Let us pray for all families throughout the world.

Gracious Father, you bless the family and renew your people. Enrich husbands and wives, parents and children more and more with your grace, that, strengthening and supporting each other, they may serve those in need and be a sign of the fulfillment of your perfect kingdom, where, with your Son Jesus Christ and the Holy Spirit, you live and reign, one God through all ages of ages. *Amen.*

American Lutheran

Let us pray.

Eternal God, creator and preserver of all life, author of salvation, and giver of all grace: Look with favor upon the world you have made, and for which your Son gave his life, and especially upon this man and this woman whom you make one flesh in Holy Matrimony. *Amen.*

Give them wisdom and devotion in the ordering of their common life, that each may be to the other a strength in need, a counselor in perplexity, a comfort in sorrow, and a companion in joy. *Amen.*

Grant that their wills may be so knit together in your will, and their spirits in your Spirit, that they may grow in love and peace with you and one another all the days of their life. *Amen.*

Give them grace, when they hurt each other, to recognize and acknowledge their fault, and to seek each other's forgiveness and yours. *Amen.*

Make their life together a sign of Christ's love to this sinful and broken world, that unity may overcome estrangement, forgiveness heal guilt, and joy conquer despair. *Amen.*

Bestow on them, if it is your will, the gift and heritage of children, and the grace to bring them up to know you, to love you, and to serve you. *Amen.*

Give them such fulfillment of their mutual affection that they may reach out in love and concern for others. *Amen.*

Grant that all married persons who have witnessed these vows may find their lives strengthened and their loyalties confirmed. *Amen.*

Grant that the bonds of our common humanity, by which all your children are united one to another, and the living to the dead, may be so transformed by your grace, that your will may be done on earth as it is in heaven; where, O Father, with your Son and the Holy Spirit, you live and reign in perfect unity, now and for ever. *Amen.*

The Blessing of the Marriage

(The husband and wife kneel.)

Most gracious God, we give you thanks for your tender love in sending Jesus Christ to come among us, to be born of a human mother, and to make the way of the cross to be the way of life. We thank you, also, for consecrating the union of man and woman in his Name. By the power of your Holy Spirit, pour out the abundance of your blessing upon this man and this woman. Defend them from every enemy. Lead them into all peace. Let their love for each other be a seal upon their hearts, a mantle about their shoulders, and a crown upon their foreheads. Bless them in their work and in their companionship; in their sleeping and in their waking; in their joys and in their sorrows; in their life and in their death. Finally, in your mercy, bring them to that table where your saints feast for ever in your heavenly home; through Jesus Christ our Lord, who with you and the Holy Spirit lives and reigns, one God, for ever and ever. *Amen.*

or

O God, you have so consecrated the covenant of marriage that in it is represented the spiritual unity between Christ and his Church: Send therefore your blessing upon these your servants, that they may so love, honor, and cherish each other in faithfulness and patience, in wisdom and true godliness, that their home may be a haven of blessing and peace; through Jesus Christ our Lord, who lives and reigns with you and the Holy Spirit, one God, now and for ever. *Amen.*

Episcopal

O God, Creator and Father of us all, we thank you for the gift of life — and, in life, for the gift of marriage.

We praise you and thank you for all the joys that can come to men and women through marriage, and the blessings of home and family.

Today, especially, we think of _____ and _____ as they begin their life together as husband and wife. With them we thank you for the joy they find in each other.

(We pray for their parents, that at this moment of parting they may rejoice in their children's happiness.)

Give _____ and _____ strength, Father, to keep the vows they have made and cherish the love they share, that they may be faithful and devoted to each other.

Help them to support each other with patience, understanding and honesty.

(Teach them to be wise and loving parents of any children they may have.)

Look with favour, God, on all our homes. Defend them from every evil that may threaten them, from outside or within.

Let your Spirit so direct all of us that we may each look to the good of others in word and deed, and grow in grace as we advance in years; through Jesus Christ our Lord. *Amen.*

United Church of Canada

Let us pray.

We give thanks to you God, as we celebrate another special event of life. We thank you for our family and friends and the high moments of their lives and of ours. We thank you for the relationships which we establish as we move through life, for the ways in which they sustain, strengthen and bless us.

We celebrate your faithfulness as we conclude our worship. You have created us male and female and provided that we may be joined together as one flesh. You have given us the capability of love. You enable us to find and choose one person with whom we share a covenant. Our celebration is an acknowledgment of your creation continuing through us.

We call for your special blessing upon _____ and _____, whom we bless in your name. Help them to continue to learn of love as they grow in their relationship with each other and with you. Grant them a special quality of happiness as they establish a new home, build a new family and support each other. Enable them to have a home that is a place of blessing and of peace.

We seek your love and grace for all who are witnesses of this holy marriage. May all who share the marriage covenant be renewed as they consider this union. May each of us grow closer to you as we consider your gifts to us and the covenant we share with you. Help us to remain a community which encourages commitment to one another. We seek your blessing in the name of Jesus, the Christ, who is the source of new life. *Amen.*

Contemporary Service

Lord God, our heavenly Father, we give thanks for the moment that brings _____ and _____ together in marriage. We recognize with thanksgiving the journeys that have brought them to this time, and we celebrate with them the hopes they hold for their life together. We ask your blessing upon them, to sustain them through the difficult and uncertain times that come to every relationship. We pray that they may continue to find in each other resources which will nurture their marriage. May they continue to grow together and may their love for one another deepen with the passing years.

We give thanks for the nurture and support of family and friends. Let us, who share the circle of celebration today, be renewed in our own commitments to one another, that we may be participants in a healed and healing society.

All this we ask in the spirit we have seen in Jesus Christ our Lord. *Amen.*

Contemporary Service

14

The Lord's Prayer

The wedding prayer is frequently followed by the Lord's Prayer. We have included three versions of the Lord's Prayer (using "trespasses," using "debts" and a more modern version). It should be remembered that if the modern version is to be used it must be printed so the congregation can read it.

THE LORD'S PRAYER

Using "Trespasses"

Our Father, who art in heaven, hallowed be thy name. Thy kingdom come. Thy will be done, on earth as it is in heaven. Give us this day our daily bread. And, forgive us our trespasses as we forgive those who trespass against us. And, lead us not into temptation, but deliver us from evil. For thine is the kingdom, and the power, and the glory, forever. *Amen.*

Using "Debts"

Our Father, who art in heaven, hallowed be thy name. Thy kingdom come. Thy will be done, on earth as it is in heaven. Give us this day our daily bread. And, forgive us our debts, as we forgive our debtors. And, lead us not into temptation, but deliver us from evil. For thine is the kingdom, and the power, and the glory, forever. *Amen.*

A Modern Version

Our Father in heaven: holy be your name, your kingdom come, your will be done, on earth as in heaven. Give us to-day our daily bread. Forgive us our sins as we forgive those who sin against us. Save us in the time of trial, and deliver us from evil. For yours is the kingdom, and the power, and the glory forever. *Amen.*

United Church of Canada

15

Affirmation of The Community

In the modern age it is strikingly clear that no person or couple lives in isolation from other people. Our food, clothing and shelter come from sources far outside our personal experience. We are highly dependent upon one another.

This is true in terms of spiritual interdependence as well as of our physical needs. We know that the chances of success in any venture are increased if we have wide support and decreased if we lack it.

The affirmation of the community provides an opportunity for the congregation to say "yes" to all that they have witnessed. It is a chance to indicate their support, to offer their blessing and to remind all of the importance of the community's continuous undergirding of all human relationships.

AFFIRMATION OF THE COMMUNITY

Clergy: The marriage of _____ and _____ unites two families and creates a new one. They ask for your blessing.

Parents (or other representatives of the families, if present): We rejoice in your union, and pray God's blessing upon you.

People: In the name of Jesus Christ we love you. By his grace, we commit ourselves with you to the bonds of marriage and the Christian home.

Clergy: Will all of you, by God's grace, do everything in your power to uphold and care for these two persons in their marriage?

People: We will.

United Methodist

The parents may add their blessing with these or similar words; the wedding party may join them.

May you dwell in God's presence forever; may true and constant love preserve you.

American Lutheran

Clergy: Will all of you witnessing these promises do all in your power to uphold these two persons in their marriage?

People: We will.

Episcopal

Clergy: We have been privileged to witness a special event in the lives of _____ and _____. They have made their covenant in our presence and have indicated their intention to move through life together. We are now given the opportunity to indicate our support and affirmation of their decision.

I invite you as members of this congregation to indicate your support by answering the following questions:

Do you commit yourself to providing all of the encouragement and support possible to help _____ and _____ in their marriage?
If so, answer, "I do."

And, do you agree to do all in your power to assist _____ and _____ in the struggles which are bound to be encountered?
If so, answer, "I do."

And, do you give yourself to the ideal of living out a life of commitment, that _____ and _____ may see in you that toward which they too should strive?
If so, answer, "I do."

Contemporary Service

Clergy: Will you who have witnessed this exchange of vows between _____ and _____ so order your lives that they will be surrounded by constant love; strengthened by your wisest counsel (when it is requested); encouraged by your thoughtful concern; and instructed by your good example?

People: We will.

Clergy: The Lord God, who created our first parents and established them in marriage, establish and sustain you, that you may find delight in each other and grow in holy love until your life's end. *Amen.*

Contemporary Service

Minister: The marriage of _____ and _____ has called us together because this union touches each one of us. A new family is established in our midst, and we celebrate that new relationship with the bride and groom. Do you who are family and friends of this couple affirm your continuing support and love to _____ and _____ as they grow in their marriage? *We do.*
Do you offer to them the best of your care and counsel in their times of struggle and your celebration with them in their times of joy? *We do.*
Will you wholeheartedly accept each of them in this community and share with them the tasks of making the world a neighborhood of human care and support? *We will.*

Contemporary Service

Benedictions
and
Blessings

The ending of a worship service is typically a word which sends us back into the busy world with a reminder that we do not go alone (God is our constant companion) and we do not cease to be the people of God. It also sends us out to celebrate the covenant that we have witnessed.

The passing of the peace (see the next chapter) may be incorporated into the blessing and departure of the congregation.

God, the Father, the Son, and the Holy Spirit bless, preserve and keep you; the Lord graciously with his favor look upon you, and so fill you with all spiritual benediction and love that you may so live together in this life that in the world to come you may have life everlasting. *Amen.*

Traditional Service

The peace of God, which passes all understanding, keep your hearts and minds in the knowledge and love of God, and his Son Jesus Christ our Lord; and the blessing of God Almighty, the Father, the Son, and the Holy Spirit, be with you and remain with you always. *Amen.*

United Church of Christ

God the Eternal keep you in love with each other, so that the peace of Christ may abide in your home. Go to serve God and your neighbor in all that you do. Bear witness to the love of God in this world so that those to whom love is a stranger will find in you generous friends. The grace of the Lord Jesus Christ and the love of God and the communion of the Holy Spirit be with you all. *Amen.*

United Methodist

Almighty God, Father, Son, and Holy Spirit, keep you in his light and truth and love now and forever. *Amen.*

American Lutheran

God the Father, God the Son, God the Holy Spirit, bless, preserve, and keep you; the Lord mercifully with his favor look upon you, and fill you with all spiritual benediction and grace; that you may faithfully live together in this life, and in the age to come have life everlasting. *Amen.*

Episcopal

We have witnessed the making of a covenant. We are a people of covenant. May the covenant which we have with God be as real to us as the covenant which we celebrate to-day, and may God, who abides with us always, keep us in harmony with one another and with him. *Amen.*

Contemporary Service

Go into the world and fulfill your lives. Hold fast your ideals. Give to one another new experiences of joy. Challenge one another that you may grow.

May the love you hold for each other, now sealed in marriage, continue to mature, that your life together may be a source of strength and inspiration to the community of your family and to the wider circle of the world.

Contemporary Service

The Peace

Recent times have seen a reintroduction of an ancient act of the Christian community. The "passing of the peace"' regularly took place in gatherings of Christians when the Apostle Paul was active in ministry not long after the time of Jesus. It was very natural that people who gathered together for worship, often in secret places and under threat of death if they were discovered, would have an important attachment to one another. Their greeting became part of their ritual. They embraced one another or simply took each other's hands as they offered some word of faith or blessing. The event became formalized to include the words "the peace of God be with you" and the response "and with you."

Many Sunday gatherings of Christians now include this formula as part of the service. The passing of peace has also become increasingly popular at other special worship gatherings such as weddings. It may be included at any point in the service although it seems most logical to be used as part of the time of gathering early in the worship or as part of the time when people share blessings with one another at the completion of the service. Generally, the officiating person provides some instruction when the passing of the peace is included in the service.

THE PEACE

Clergy: The peace of the Lord be with you always.

People: And also with you.

(The couple and minister(s) may greet each other, after which greetings may be exchanged throughout the congregation.)

United Methodist

Clergy: The peace of the Lord be always with you.

People: And also with you.

(The newly married couple then greet each other, after which greetings may be exchanged through the congregation.)

Episcopal

THE PEACE

Clergy: I invite you to greet one another in the name and spirit of the risen Lord. Will you turn to someone near you and say "the peace of God be yours" or some other appropriate greeting.

(The couple and people greet one another.)

Clergy: I send you out as people of peace. May the God of peace be yours. *Amen.*

Contemporary Service

Part III
Special Services

The Civil Ceremony
(for Justices of the Peace, Judges, Notaries, Etc.)

For many years the option of a wedding outside of church has been available to couples. This option allows a couple to go to a justice of the peace, an attorney or other person legally qualified to solemnize a marriage.

All of the material in this book is available to the person officiating at a civil ceremony. He or she may simply choose from the various options and put together a service that seems appropriate. As with the clergy, those officiating at civil ceremonies may ask couples to choose the options which they prefer for their service.

However, a civil ceremony with less religious language may be preferred. In order to provide such an alternative model the following two civil ceremonies are offered.

A CIVIL CEREMONY

The officiating person, witnesses and the couple to be married gather and exchange these words:

Presiding Person: We are here to participate in a wedding. By this act we unite _____ and _____ as husband and wife. What we do today is done in conformity to the laws of the state of _____ and in the tradition of men and women of all places and times.

_____ and _____, you stand before me having requested that I marry you. Do you both do this of your own free will, with no pressure upon you from other persons?

Man and Woman: We do.

Presiding Person: Do any of the witnesses know of any reason why we may not legally continue with this wedding?

Witnesses: We do not.

Presiding Person: Then let us continue. _____, if it is your desire to become the husband of _____, then repeat after me:

I, _____, take you, _____, to be my wife. In this moment I promise before these witnesses to love you and care for you for all of our days. I accept you with your faults and your strengths, even as I offer myself with my faults and strengths. I promise to support you when you need support and to turn to you when I need support. I choose you as the one with whom I will spend my life.

Presiding Person: _____, if it is your desire to become the wife of _____, then repeat after me:

I, _____, take you, _____, to be my husband. In this moment I promise before these witnesses to love you and care for you for all of our days. I accept you with your faults and your strengths, even as I offer myself with my faults and strengths. I promise to support you when you need support and to turn to you when I need support. I choose you as the one with whom I will spend my life.

Presiding Person: _____ and _____, you have shared promises in our presence. Do you have a token or symbol which you wish to exchange?

Couple: We do.

Presiding Person: _____, will you give your token to _____ and repeat these words:

I give you this ring as a constant reminder of the promises we exchanged today. As you receive this ring, receive my promise of faithfulness to you.

_____, will you give your token to _____ and repeat these words:

I give you this ring as a constant reminder of the promises we exchanged today. As you receive this ring, receive my promise of faithfulness to you.

Presiding Person: _____ and _____, you have exchanged your promises and given and received tokens in my presence. By these acts you have become husband and wife. According to the laws of the state of _____, I hereby pronounce that you are husband and wife. You may seal your promise with a kiss.

A CIVIL WEDDING

Presiding Person: Friends, we have come together today to witness the marriage of _____ and _____ . The legal requirements of this state having been fulfilled, and the license for their marriage being present, I must ask of each party if they come of their own free will and accord.

(To the Man) _____ , do you come to this union of your free will, and with the intention of being faithful in marriage to _____ as long as you shall live? *I do.*

(To the Woman) _____ , do you come to this union of your free will, and with the intention of being faithful in marriage to _____ as long as you shall live? *I do.*

Presiding Person: Who presents _____ to be married to _____ ?

Bride's Father (or other representative): I do.

Presiding Person:

(To the Man) Please repeat the following after me:

I, _____ , do take you, _____ , to be my lawfully wedded wife. I promise from this day forward to be your faithful husband, for better for worse, for richer for poorer, in sickness and in health, to love and to cherish, as long as I shall live.

(To the Woman) Please repeat the following after me:

I, _____ , do take you, _____ , to be my lawfully wedded husband. I promise from this day forward to be your faithful wife, for better for worse, for richer for poorer, in sickness and in health, to love and to cherish, as long as I shall live.

The wedding ring seals the vows of marriage as a signature bears witness to a written covenant. As the ring is placed upon the finger, will you repeat these words:

Man and Woman: In pledge of the vow of marriage made between us, I offer you this ring. Let it be to you and to me, and to all the world, the symbol of the covenant of marriage we have accepted.

Presiding Person: We who have come together in this place have heard the willingness of _____ and _____ to be joined in marriage. They have come of their free will and in our hearing have made a covenant of faithfulness. They have given and received a ring as the seal of their promises.

Therefore, by the power vested in me by this state I pronounce that they are husband and wife.

The Roman Catholic and Ecumenical Wedding

One of the authors was once invited to an ecumenical wedding of a young man who was a member of his church. The man was marrying a young woman who was a Roman Catholic. It was a moving service which included appropriate scripture lessons, a well-worded meditation by the pastor, music which truly enriched the experience and prayers that moved the congregation in beseeching God.

The author left the service celebrating the rich worship of the Roman Catholic Church and bemoaning the simple service which had become traditional in some Protestant circles. Within a matter of weeks work began on this book.

The Catholic Church as been several steps ahead of most Protestant denominations in the preparation of written resources for use by people getting married. A number of fine books have been written to help Catholics understand the wedding service and choose the parts of their own wedding. We have decided not to duplicate that material in this book. It is available from most priests and can be used along with this book if an ecumenical wedding is desired. However it seems important to share an outline of the Roman Catholic marriage rite as it is most often used. Normally the format for the rite for marriage during mass will be:

Entrance (Procession)

Liturgy of the Word
  Old Testament
  Epistle
  Gospel
  Homily (Sermon)

Rite of Marriage
  Statement of Purpose
  Questions of Willingness and Consent
  Exchange of Vows
  Blessing and Exchange of Rings

Liturgy of the Eucharist
  The order of the mass is followed with modifications
    suited to the wedding rite
  The Lord's Prayer
  Nupial Blessing
  Blessing at the End of Mass

Little needs to be said about the rich resources which are brought into any act of worship by the tradition of the Roman Catholic Church. The reverent spirit and colorful pageantry which have long been among the gifts of the Catholic Church are more and more accessible to the entire Christian community, and all of us are made richer for the sharing. As the mass has been, for some years now, spoken in the language of the congregation, the language of faith is more a shared expression and makes possible ecumenical communication at an increasing deep level. While Protestants and Catholics have a long way to go still, it is possible now to participate together in worship in ways which were unheard of only a few years ago.

In this time of ever-shrinking divisions among Christians of various denominational backgrounds, we see growing numbers of ecumenical weddings. What was once a rare occurrence is now frequent. In this light one must have some basic considerations.

First, one must never underestimate the importance of his or her spiritual roots. This is particularly relevant when it comes to planning a wedding for a marriage which will bring together two strong spiritual traditions.

In order to keep peace there is often the temptation to say: "Religion is not all that important. One or the other of us can change without any problem." While it may be possible for some to change religious affiliation as one changes a sweater, for most of us it is undesirable if not impossible to remove the spiritual traditions of childhood and family. One's religious roots nurture how we see ourselves personally and within the community. They are a source of personal ethics and social behavior. They make a difference in the way we think about and plan for having children and how we go about educating children in the ideas that give our life meaning. These roots are so deep in us we are scarcely aware of them until, sometimes, they break out onto the surface in explosive and surprising ways. All of us have seen the heartbreak when a mixed marriage is begun with little consideration of the bride's and groom's religious traditions but is driven apart at a later time because of these differences.

The issue of changing one's religion, even in the name of love and devotion, is a painful one. It is an issue which must involve long and loving conversation and patience on both sides. The inner struggle in each partner will test the strength of his or her commitment to each other. Each person has the right and responsibility in a marriage to bring his or her spiritual perspective into the union. Neither has a right to expect or demand of the other a concession of those ideas or understandings which are basic and important. Hopefully, neither party will give up his or her religious affiliation in order to be married.

This suggestion is not intended in any way to suggest that a man and woman need not make every effort to work out common understandings about religious questions. It is important, so far as possible, to affirm the great gifts of each tradition in developing a new and inclusive family outlook. We encourage you to do everything possible to ground your marriage in mutual religious support. Let your religious affiliations be supportive of your new and enduring relationship, and, if concessions seem necessary, let there be a balance between the bride's traditions and those of the groom.

But, above all, do not allow the wedding ceremony to be the occasion for the renouncing of one's childhood or family faith. It is not a good burden to place upon a marriage.

Another suggestion which has to do with ecumenical weddings is rather obvious and yet bears mentioning. Whenever possible, with the permission of the host pastor, invite the second clergyman or -woman to participate in the wedding. It always enriches the wedding to have both faiths represented by clergy and to give both families a sense of involvement and support. The act of guest clergy participation can be either symbolic or central to the wedding. In some cases a minister or priest offers a brief prayer or some other word of blessing. In other cases a sermon or meditation can be given by the guest. Or the various parts of the service can be divided by the two participants.

Still another consideration of ecumenical weddings is the matter of the specific words of the wedding. It can often be important to the bride or groom, as well as to both of the families involved, that some expression of their particular faith be included in the service. If, for example, either member of the wedding party is Jewish, an Old Testament lesson should certainly be included. If one party is Roman Catholic thought should be given to how the Lord's Prayer is to be said.

The key to making worship meaningful in an ecumenical wedding is *consideration*. If the clergyman or -woman is aware of the religious background of the couple and their families, he or she will normally make every effort to make the service meet the needs of all involved. It is an unusual pastor who ignores the spiritual needs of people who are worshipping in his or her church.

20

The Jewish Wedding Ceremony

The roots of Christian wedding ceremonies are deeply inter-woven with the much older Jewish traditions. Based in deep com-mitment to the values of home and family, the Jewish ceremony is rich in ancient wisdom which makes clear the responsibilities of husband and wife not only to one another but also to the larger com-munity. The covenant of marriage between man and woman sym-bolizes, for the Jewish as for the Christian community, the love of God for creation and God's faithfulness.

The Jewish wedding ceremony, performed in the presence of two official witnesses, includes two essential elements: betrothal and blessing.

In the former, the groom places the ring upon the finger of the bride with these words:

"Be sanctified to me with this ring in accordance with the law of Moses and Israel."

Customarily the wedding ring is a simple band, unadorned with precious stones, symbolizing the pure motivation of the groom in offering this gift and the fact that its full value is visible (that is, un-enhanced or diminished in value by the addition of embellishment). It is a strongly held tradition that the ring offered the bride be owned by the groom and be neither borrowed nor otherwise encumbered. More than a symbol of covenant, the ring is a gift to the bride, and she may consider it her personal property.

Having received the wedding ring, the bride indicates her consent to betrothal, the covenant between the bride and groom is established and the betrothal is complete.

The second part of the ceremony now begins as the bride and groom stand together beneath the canopy, or covering, as the Seven Benedictions are recited. During this recital the bride and groom drink from a common cup of wine, hear or read the wedding contract which has been earlier arranged and, finally, break the wine glass, symbolizing the destruction of Jerusalem and the community's hope for its restoration.

While there is wide variation within Judaism, an order for a Jewish wedding ceremony will generally include:

Opening Scriptural Sentences

A Prayer Invoking God's Presence

An Address by the Rabbi

The Statement of the Marriage Covenant

The Seven Benedictions

The Blessing and Sharing of Wine

The Ring Ceremony

The Wedding Declaration or Pronouncement

Silent Prayer

The Benediction.

It should be noted that marriage between Jews and non-Jews has not been generally recognized under Jewish law and has not been considered valid in the Jewish community. A mixed marriage in which one partner is Jewish and the other is not has been considered to be in violation of the basic understanding of Jewish marriage and family life.

It is also true, however, that our age is a time when differences of religion do not necessarily keep couples from developing relationships which may lead to marriage.

More and more we can expect interfaith weddings to take place. It is important when this happens to honor the traditions of each member of the wedding party as far as possible. The expressions of both faiths can add greatly to the beauty of the wedding ceremony and may be helpful in developing avenues of communication between bride and groom and between the families of each.

It may be helpful to remember that more than one element of the ceremony may be duplicated as a means of affirming two distinct traditions. There may be, for example, two exchanges of vows, one from each tradition. One may embody the Jewish elements and fulfill the requirements of that religious community while the other may represent a Christian perspective. The ceremony should express a sense of wholeness and unity, but it must also satisfy members of both religious traditions that their respective spiritual needs have been met.

The benefits which come from a ceremony which brings together successfully the resources of two faiths will far outweigh the problems which may be associated with planning such an event. Altogether too many couples sacrifice a significant chance to grow in the name of "making it easier" for both families. To compromise one's spiritual foundations or to abandon them completely may result in a ceremony which is unsatisfying to one person or the other and healing for neither. We urge you to do your best, working with the people who will officiate at your interfaith wedding, to be sure the ceremony does everything possible to offer an affirmation of the best of both ancient traditions.

That said, let us stress that most Jewish rabbis will not approve mixed marriages or interfaith ceremonies. They may regard it as a mockery and an affront to both communities. The same may be true of some Christian ministers.

21

Writing
Your Own Service

Having looked through this book, and having thought about some of the rich traditional and more contemporary words which are available for your wedding, you may still wish to write your own service — or some major segment of it. We encourage you to give this possibility careful thought in order that the ceremony which you develop represents the best of your vision for your marriage. You may think of the portions of the wedding service which you write as important gifts to those present, especially to the one you are marrying, and you will want to choose your words as carefully as you would chose a more tangible gift.

As you begin to gather resources for your service, it is essential that you bear in mind that some parts of the wedding ceremony are necessary if the occasion is to be a *wedding*. These essentials are:

1. the vows you make to each other;
2. the announcement by the "official witness" — your minister, priest, rabbi or other authorized official — that the words and symbols have been exchanged in his or her presence.

With this simple formula the wedding ceremony is complete, legal and binding. But you may want your wedding to include much more.

Some of the questions you will want to keep in mind as you develop your plans are:

- What do we want to say about the marriage relationship in our wedding ceremony?
- What do we dream for ourselves and for each other through marriage?
- How can we put those thoughts into words for our wedding?

As you work with the answers to these questions, you may see a pattern emerging — a sense of direction for further work. Beginning to put together some of the parts of the ceremony, as one puts a puzzle together, will help you to identify a theme or thread.

You may remember a line of poetry that has long been a treasure to you because it speaks of love in a way that seems to fit your feelings. That line may find its way into your service. And you may look through books of poetry in the library to discover some of the traditional and more recent reflections on the meaning of relationships. Enjoy the searching.

Certainly you will want to talk at an early stage with the officiating person about your desire to write a part or all of your service. That person too will be a helpful resource. Often pastors who have been long involved with wedding plans maintain a file of the ideas couples have shared with them in the past. Most people who are in the ministry will be supportive of your thinking and will encourage conversations about the writing of your service.

You may discover that you may have gathered some ideas

that just do not fit into the ceremony you are planning. This will be an affirmation that you are sharpening the focus of your plans. Some words or ideas may seem good in themselves but just do not fit in *your* wedding. There are also some materials that are simply in poor taste, and you will reject them on those grounds. Remember that you want your wedding to reflect the very best of your thinking. Consultation with the minister, as well as with family and close friends, will help you achieve this.

Finally, attention should be given to the format in which the ceremony, if you write it, will be provided to the person officiating. It is very difficult for a smooth ceremony to be conducted if the minister has to shuffle pages of differing sizes and shapes. It is the responsibility of the couple who create the service to make a clean, neat and easy-to-handle copy of the entire ceremony and to provide this for the person who officiates. It is a good idea to consult him or her about the format which he or she prefers.

Renewal of Wedding Vows

It is increasingly common for couples to decide to renew their wedding vows on the occasion of an anniversary. This special moment is an affirmation of their relationship and of the values which have been the foundation of their life together. It can be a time of great warmth and celebration as family and friends gather to celebrate the memory of the first vows.

Some suggestions are offered in planning such an event:

1. Couples are urged to take an active part in putting together the various components of their service of renewal. All of the choices found in this book may be appropriate, although in many cases it will be necessary for the person officiating or the couple to make a few editorial changes to make the service exactly fit the situation.

2. All of the possibilities for special music, processional music, flowers, etc., are available for a renewal of vows service. The simplicity or complexity of the event should be determined by the couple involved.

Most of these services, however, tend to be rather simple and do not involve many people beyond the family.

3. Creative possibilities sometimes help to simplify such an event. It is possible, for example, for the husband and wife to enter the sanctuary together and walk down the aisle arm in arm as they approach the ceremony. It may well be that attempts to duplicate closely the service of years ago will lend a phony quality to the event and will take away far more than they add.

4. Participants should look for ways to make the event warm and personal rather than formal and impersonal. It is a celebration of years spent together and a renewal of promises for coming years. What could be more warm and personal?

Our Blessing

The most satisfying blessings at a wedding come as a result of the couple's own effort and dedication. Your work in planning and developing your wedding service will result in blessings which will extend far beyond the moment of the wedding and to others besides yourselves.

Those who are your honored guests will be blessed. The service will speak to them of your relationship. The presence of God will enrich them and give them confidence in the covenant which you make on your wedding day. And they will see, if not discover, your rich spiritual natures as they experience and participate in a worship service which the two of you have created.

Perhaps the most exciting blessing, however, is the one which comes to the two of you as you recall and relive the moments of your wedding day. You will be blessed by the pleasant memories of reading this book to make your choices. You will be blessed as you reflect on the comments of your friends and family about the service. And you will be blessed as you recall the words which you chose and how they reflected your love and commitment to one another.

We take this opportunity to add our blessing to those of many others who wish you well in your wedding and your future. This book, with its wide range of offerings from various denominations, augmented with our own contributions, is seen by us as a gift to every couple planning a wedding service.